勇 虎 爱 忠 勤

Spotlight on China

Robin Johnson & Bobbie Kalman

Crabtree Publishing Company

www.crabtreebooks.com

勇 虎 爱 忠 勤

Spotlight On My Country

Created by Bobbie Kalman

For Jeniah Wiens
You are a beautiful gift from China!

Editor-in-Chief
Bobbie Kalman

Writing team
Robin Johnson
Bobbie Kalman

Editor
Michael Hodge

Photo research
Bobbie Kalman
Robin Johnson
Crystal Sikkens

Design
Katherine Berti

Production coordinator
Katherine Berti

Illustrations
Barbara Bedell: page 11
Lauren Fast: page 18 (top)
Rose Gowsell: page 28 (yin-yang)
Katherine Berti: pages 4, 5
Robert MacGregor: page 18 (bottom)

Photographs
© Dreamstime.com: pages 7 (middle right inset and bottom right inset), 11 (middle), 29 (top left)
© iStockphoto.com: pages 9 (bottom), 11 (top)
© 2008 Jupiterimages Corporation: pages 4, 7 (background and top left inset), 8, 12, 17, 20
© Bobbie Kalman: page 13 (top)
© Shutterstock.com: cover, pages 1, 3, 5, 6, 7 (bottom left inset), 9 (top), 10, 13 (bottom), 14, 15, 18, 19, 21, 22, 23, 24, 25, 26 (middle and bottom), 27, 28 (except yin-yang), 29 (top right and bottom), 30 (except bottom left), 31 (top)
© en.wikipedia: Tee Meng: page 30 (bottom left); PENG, Yanan: page 26 (top)
Other images by Corel and Digital Stock

Library and Archives Canada Cataloguing in Publication

Johnson, Robin (Robin R.)
Spotlight on China / Robin Johnson & Bobbie Kalman.

(Spotlight on my country)
Includes index.
ISBN 978-0-7787-3454-3 (bound).--ISBN 978-0-7787-3480-2 (pbk.)

1. China--Juvenile literature. I. Kalman, Bobbie, 1947- II. Title. III. Series.

DS706.J64 2008 j951 C2008-901025-6

Library of Congress Cataloging-in-Publication Data

Johnson, Robin (Robin R.)
Spotlight on China / Robin Johnson and Bobbie Kalman.
p. cm. -- (Spotlight on my country)
Includes index.
ISBN-13: 978-0-7787-3454-3 (rlb)
ISBN-10: 0-7787-3454-4 (rlb)
ISBN-13: 978-0-7787-3480-2 (pb)
ISBN-10: 0-7787-3480-3 (pb)
1. China--Juvenile literature. I. Kalman, Bobbie. II. Title.
DS706.J58 2008
951--dc22

2008005107

Crabtree Publishing Company
www.crabtreebooks.com 1-800-387-7650

Printed in Canada/082019/CH20190711

Published in Canada
Crabtree Publishing
616 Welland Ave.
St. Catharines, Ontario
L2M 5V6

Published in the United States
Crabtree Publishing
PMB 59051
350 Fifth Avenue, 59th Floor
New York, New York 10118

Published in the United Kingdom
Crabtree Publishing
Maritime House
Basin Road North, Hove
BN41 1WR

Published in Australia
Crabtree Publishing
Unit 3 – 5
Currumbin Court
Capalaba QLD 4157

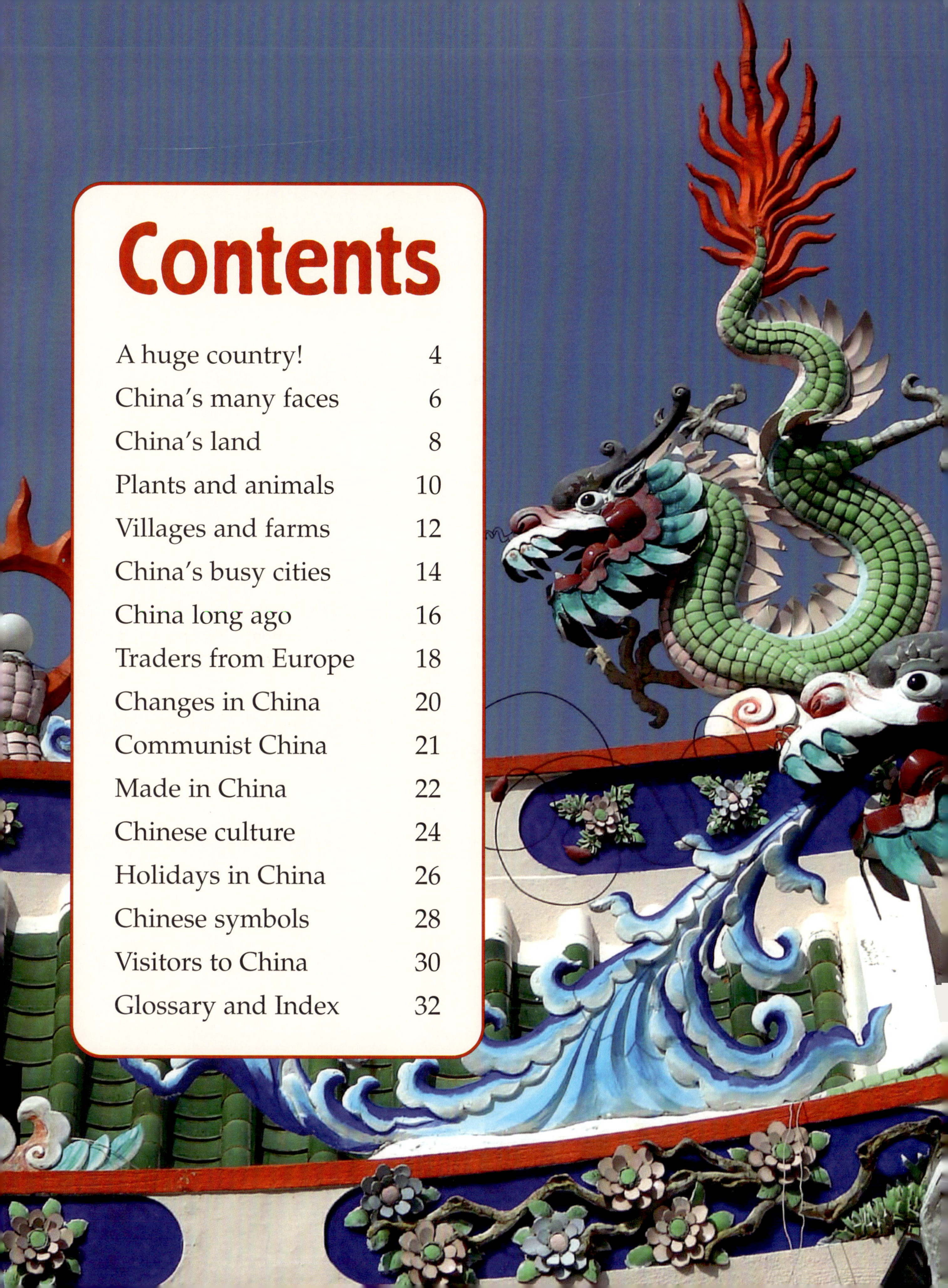

Contents

A huge country!

Welcome to China! China is one of the biggest **countries** on Earth. A country is an area of land that has people. China has more people than any other country! A country has **laws**, or rules, that its people must follow. A country also has **borders.** Borders separate countries from their neighbors. Find China's neighbors on the map below. There are fourteen!

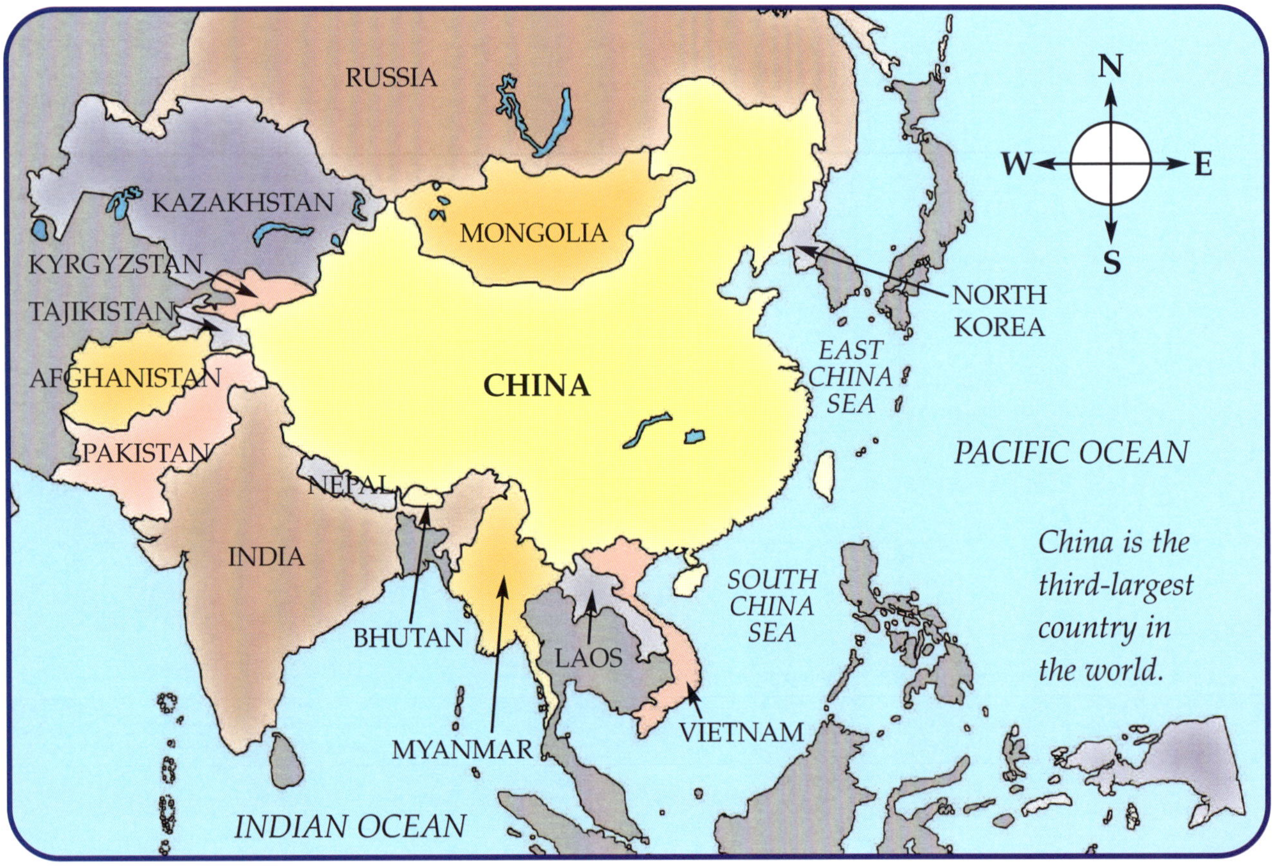

China is the third-largest country in the world.

Where on Earth is China?

China is part of the **continent** of Asia. A continent is a huge area of land. There are seven continents on Earth. Asia is the largest continent. The other continents are North America, South America, Europe, Africa, Australia and Oceania, and Antarctica. The continents are shown on the map below.

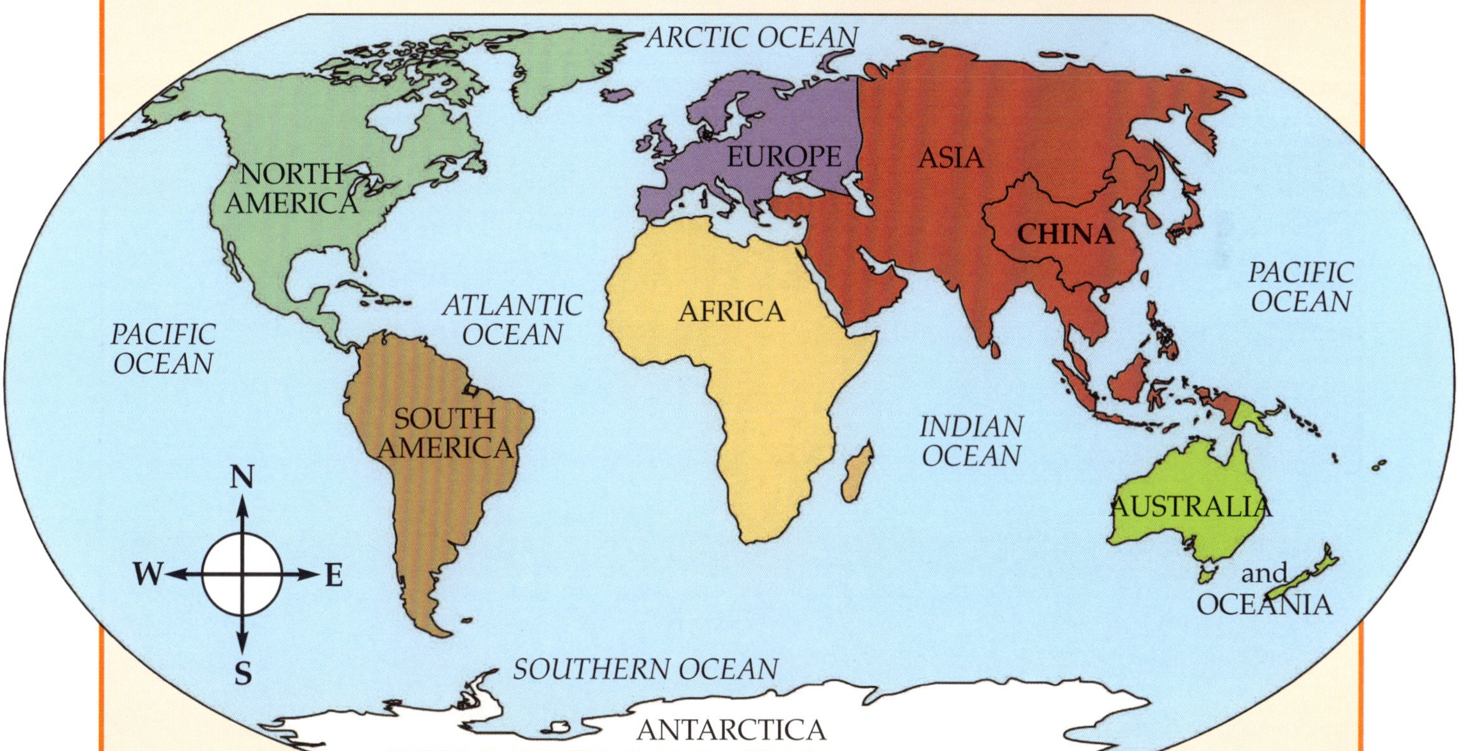

Which other continents does Asia touch?

China's many faces

China has a lot of people! The **population** of China is over 1.4 billion. Population is the number of people who live in a country. People who live in China are called Chinese. Most Chinese speak Mandarin. It is the **official language** of the country.

One-child family

The **government** of China is trying to stop its population from growing. It does this by rewarding families who have only one child. One-child families receive money and better homes. Families with more than one child are punished. They must pay **fines**, or money, to the government. In some places, two children are allowed.

More than one-sixth of the world's people live in China!

National groups

Most Chinese people are Han Chinese, but there are 56 **national groups** in China. National groups are groups of people who share languages, beliefs, customs, and **religions**. The people of each of these groups live very different lives.

The people on this page may not look like they are from one country, but they are all Chinese!

China's land

China's land can be divided into three **regions**, or areas. The **landscapes** in each region are very different. A landscape is how land looks. In western China, there are high mountains and **plateaus**. In the **central**, or middle, region of China, there are smaller mountains and huge **deserts**. On the eastern coast of China, there are **plains**. Plains are flat areas of land that have very few trees.

High in western China's mountains, the ***climate*** *is cold and snowy. Climate is the usual weather in an area. Some of Earth's highest mountains are in this region. Animals called yaks are raised here for their milk, hair, and meat. Yaks also carry heavy loads. This baby yak is drinking its mother's milk.*

On China's plains, the climate is warm and wet. The land is ***fertile****. Fertile means that the soil is good for growing plants. Most of the people in China live in this region.*

The climate in China's deserts is very hot and dry. Huge ***dunes****, or hills of sand, are shaped by the wind. These people are riding camels through a desert in China.*

Plants and animals

peony

There are thousands of kinds of plants and animals in China. The plants and animals grow or live in different regions of the country. They are suited to the places and climates where they live. Some of China's plants and animals are shown on these pages.

Peonies are popular flowering plants in China. They are grown in Chinese gardens and are used in Chinese medicines.

Giant pandas live in forests on China's central mountains. The pandas eat mainly ***bamboo****. Bamboo is a woody grass that grows in this cool, wet area. These pandas are eating bamboo.*

Chinese alligators live in ***swamps*** *on China's coast. Swamps are flat, wet areas with many plants. The alligators eat fish and other animals that live in the swamp waters.*

Bactrian camels live in China's desert region. There is very little water in the desert, so few plants grow there. Camels can live several days without eating or drinking.

Animals in danger

Over one hundred kinds of animals live only in China. Sadly, many of these animals are **endangered**. Endangered animals are in danger of dying out in the **wild**. Giant pandas, Chinese alligators, Bactrian camels, and South China tigers are all endangered animals.

This tiger is a South China tiger. Scientists believe that there are fewer than 30 South China tigers left in the wild.

Villages and farms

More than half of China's people live in **villages**. A village is a small town in the countryside. In China's villages, grandparents, parents, and children often live together. The families also work together on farms. They sell their **crops** and other goods at nearby markets. Crops are plants that are grown to be used by people. Rice and wheat are crops.

*Most village homes are crowded with many family members. The homes do not have running water or heating. People get water from **wells** and do their laundry in nearby rivers or lakes.*

Farming for food

Many Chinese are farmers. Farmers in China grow rice, wheat, corn, potatoes, tea, peanuts, cotton, and many other crops. Rice is the most important crop. Farmers have grown rice for thousands of years. It is a **staple** food for most Chinese families. A staple food is eaten every day.

These girls are enjoying tasty bowls of soup made with rice noodles and vegetables.

Farming in China is hard work! Much of the work is done by hand. Farmers spend many hours in the fields each day. These farmers are working in rice ***paddies****, or fields. Rice paddies are very wet!*

China's busy cities

Many Chinese live in cities. China's cities are busy places! They have many restaurants, shops, schools, and factories. The **capital** of China is Beijing. A capital is the city in which a country's main government is located.

There are many beautiful buildings in Beijing. This building is called the Temple of Heaven.

Beijing is crowded with people and cars. Almost thirteen million people live in Beijing!

Most people use bicycles to travel through China's crowded city streets.

Shanghai is the biggest city in China. Boats carry many goods into and out of this busy city.

China long ago

A great civilization

People have lived in China for thousands of years. China is one of the oldest **civilizations** on Earth. A civilization is a group of people that shares languages, government, religion, and a way of telling their history. The Chinese people of long ago studied art and science. They grew crops for food. They traded goods with other civilizations. They were ruled by **dynasties**, or powerful families. An **emperor** was the head of a dynasty. The picture on the opposite page is from the time of the Tang Dynasty.

The Forbidden City was built during the Ming Dynasty. The Emperor of China lived and worked in the Forbidden City. Members of the Chinese government also worked there. All others were ***forbidden****, or not allowed, to go near the palace gates.*

Traders from Europe

Marco Polo

In the 1200s, an Italian explorer named Marco Polo traveled to China. He spent many years exploring and learning about the country. In later years, explorers and traders from many other countries came to China. They wanted Chinese silks, teas, spices, and **porcelain**. They fought to control China, its trading, and its treasures.

This vase is made of porcelain.

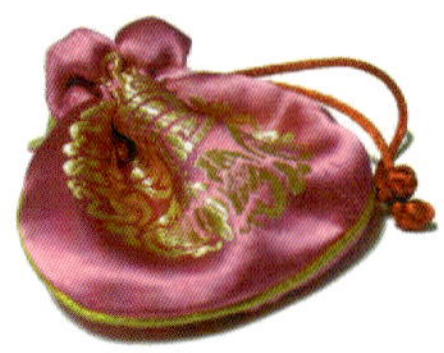

This pouch is made of silk.

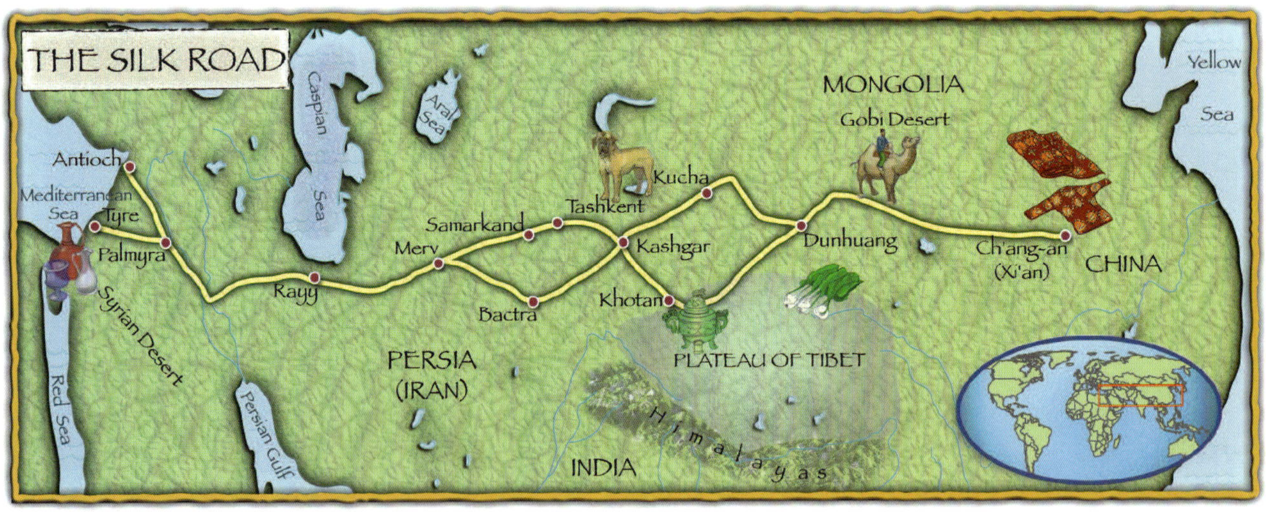

*Traders and explorers traveled on the **Silk Road** to China. The Chinese built the Silk Road to bring traders from countries in Asia and Europe to China. Long ago, silk was a very valuable material. The Chinese traded silk for gold, silver, and gemstones.*

A British colony

In 1842, the island of Hong Kong became a British **colony**. A colony is an area that is ruled by a faraway country. In 1997, Hong Kong was returned to China. Today, Hong Kong is very different from the rest of China. It has Chinese and British ways. Both Chinese and English languages are spoken there. Hong Kong is a very modern city with many **skyscrapers**, or tall buildings.

This boat is sailing in Victoria Harbour in Hong Kong. Victoria Harbour is named after a British queen. The boat is a Chinese boat. Hong Kong has a blend of Chinese and British ways.

Changes in China

By the early 1900s, a few rich, powerful people owned all the land in China. They forced Chinese farmers to work hard for little pay. Most of the people of China were very poor and unhappy. In 1911, a man named Sun Yat-sen and his followers forced the Chinese emperor to give up his power. China became a **democratic republic**. In a democratic republic, the citizens of a country choose their leader. The citizens of China chose Sun Yat-sen to be their first **president**.

Yat-sen promised to give land to Chinese farmers.

Communist China

Sun Yat-sen was not able to bring the people of China together or to solve all of their problems. There was fighting in China for many years. In 1949, a man named Mao Zedong became the new leader of China. China became a **communist** country with a new name—the People's Republic of China.

What is communism?
In a communist country, the government makes most of the decisions for the people of the country. It decides which crops are grown on farms, which products are made in factories, and where people will live. People cannot choose their leaders or decide how their country should be run. Many people do not feel free, and they do not feel safe.

Made in China

It took many years for China's **economy** to improve. Economy is the way a country uses its money, goods, and **services**. In the early 1980s, the Chinese government began allowing people to keep the money they earned. People in China can now own land and run their own businesses. They can sell goods in China and to other countries.

In the past, everything that was made in China belonged to the government. Farmers could not sell the crops they grew and keep the money. Today, farmers can sell their own crops. People who own shops, restaurants, and other businesses can also sell their goods and services.

A booming economy

Today, China's economy is **booming**, or doing very well. China is the second-largest **exporter** in the world. An exporter sells goods to other countries. Many of the things that we buy in stores come from China. Look around your home. How many of the things that you own were made in China?

Many of your toys were made in China.

Some Chinese people can now afford to buy computers, cell phones, cars, and even large homes.

Chinese culture

For many years, the people of China were not allowed to dance, create art or music, or play sports. Today, they can celebrate their **culture** again. Culture is the beliefs, customs, and ways of life that are shared by a group of people. China's culture is a colorful mix of old and modern ways.

For hundreds of years, the people of China practiced ***martial arts****. Martial arts were once used in fighting. Today, they are mainly for fun, fitness, and sport. People all over the world now practice Chinese martial arts.*

Opera *is a traditional form of entertainment in China. An opera is a musical play. In Chinese opera, there is singing, dancing, and pretend fighting. The opera singers wear fancy costumes and makeup.*

Chinese artists have painted pictures on paper and silk since long ago. Many artists are also skilled in **calligraphy**. Calligraphy is the art of fine handwriting. This young woman is looking at her calligraphy. She is pleased with the words she has painted.

(above) Ping-pong is the most popular sport in China. It is played in homes, parks, and school yards across the country.

(left) ***Acrobatics*** *have been a part of Chinese culture for over two thousand years. Today, Chinese gymnasts perform acrobatics in shows and circuses around the world.*

Holidays in China

The people of China celebrate their culture with many lively **festivals**. A festival is a special event or celebration. Some important Chinese festivals are shown on these pages.

On October 1, Chinese celebrate ***National Day****. This holiday honors the creation of the People's Republic of China. On this day, people from across the country gather in Beijing for a huge parade. Afterwards, they go to the Forbidden City for singing, dancing, and fireworks.*

The ***Dragon Boat Festival*** *is usually held in June. During this fun festival, teams race dragon boats. A dragon boat is a long, thin boat that holds up to 70 people. Fans cheer and wave colorful flags.*

Chinese New Year

The most important holiday in China is **Chinese New Year**. The Chinese celebrate this week-long holiday at the end of January or the beginning of February. During Chinese New Year, people visit their friends and families. They wear new clothing and give young people red envelopes filled with money. There are many parades, feasts, and fireworks throughout this special holiday.

A Chinese New Year parade always has a lion dance. This white lion is made up of two people. Lions guard people and keep them safe.

勇 虎 爱 忠 勤

Chinese symbols

There are many **symbols** in Chinese culture. A symbol is a picture that **represents**, or stands for, an object or idea. Some Chinese symbols and their meanings are shown on these pages.

This is the flag of the People's Republic of China. The big yellow star stands for the communist leaders in China. The four small stars represent the people of China.

*The **yin-yang** is a very old Chinese symbol. It represents opposites working together in life.*

Chinese dragons represent power. They have been used in Chinese stories and art for thousands of years. People perform dragon dances during festivals and make boats in the shapes of dragons.

In Chinese culture, the color red represents wealth, happiness, success, and many other good things. Red paper is used to wrap gifts of money. Chinese brides wear red wedding dresses, and the tables at their weddings are set with red tablecloths and napkins. The Double Happiness characters are placed where the bride and groom can see them.

DOUBLE HAPPINESS

Picture this!

The Chinese language is made up of thousands of symbols called **pictographs**. Each pictograph represents an entire word. Some Mandarin pictographs are shown in the picture on the right.

Visitors to China

Millions of tourists visit China each year. Tourists are people who travel to places for fun. Even more tourists from around the world traveled to Beijing, China, to watch the Summer **Olympics** in 2008. Many new hotels, shops, and restaurants were built for the Olympics. These new services continue to promote tourism in China.

This colorful statue was made for the Beijing Olympics. The five rings are a symbol of the Olympic Games.

*Many **stadiums**, hotels, and other buildings have been built for the Olympics. This is a picture of Beijing National Stadium.*

*The **slogan** for the 2008 Olympics was "One World, One Dream."*

While in China, tourists can explore the Yangtze River in a ***sampan****. A sampan is a flat-bottomed boat. The Yangtze River is the longest river in Asia and the third-longest river in the world!*

The ***Great Wall of China*** *is the most popular place to visit in China. This huge stone wall was built long ago to protect the Chinese from enemies. It is the largest human-made structure on Earth.*

Glossary

Note: Some boldfaced words are defined where they appear in the book.

acrobatics Stunts that need to be performed with skill and balance

desert An area that receives very little rain

dynasty A series of rulers from the same family and the period of time during which they ruled

government A group of people who are in charge of a country and who make important decisions and laws that its citizens must follow

official language The language used in government and business and which children are taught in school

Olympics Sporting events in which athletes from many countries compete

plateau Flat land that is on high ground

porcelain A type of fine pottery

president The leader of a country

religion A set of beliefs about God or gods

service The act of helping or doing work for others

slogan A phrase or group of words used by a certain person, organization, or business

stadium A structure made up of rows of seats built around a field

staple A main crop that is grown, such as wheat or rice, which is eaten every day

well A deep hole in the ground from which people get water

wild The natural places that are not controlled by people

Index